Photo by Richard C. Trigg

Bernadette Sullivan and Mark Shannon in a scene from the Actors Theatre of Louisville production of "Down the Road." Set design by Paul Owen.

# DOWN THE ROAD

BY LEE BLESSING

★

★

DRAMATISTS
PLAY SERVICE
INC.

*For Jeanne Blake*

DOWN THE ROAD was first produced at La Jolla Playhouse (Des McAnuff, Artistic Director; Alan Levy, Managing Director) in La Jolla, California, on August 8, 1989. It was directed by Des McAnuff; the scene design was by Neil Patel; the costume design was by Susan Hilferty; the lighting design was by Peter Maradudin; the sound design was by John Kilgore and the original music was by Michael Roth. The cast was as follows:

DAN HENNIMAN ...............................................Jonathan Hogan
IRIS HENNIMAN ...................................................Susan Berman
WILLIAM REACH ..................................................James Morrison


DOWN THE ROAD was presented at the Actors Theatre of Louisville (Jon Jory, Producing Director) at the Fifteenth Annual Humana Festival of New American Plays, in Louisville, Kentucky, on March 6, 1991. It was directed by Jeanne Blake; the scene design was by Paul Owen; the costume design was by Hollis Jenkins-Evans; the lighting design was by Mary Louise Geiger; the sound design was by Darron West and the production stage manager was Debra Acquavella. The cast was as follows:

DAN HENNIMAN ...................................................Mark Shannon
IRIS HENNIMAN ...........................................Bernadette Sullivan
WILLIAM REACH .............................................Markus Flanagan

4

# CHARACTERS

IRIS HENNIMAN — early 30s, free-lance writer

DAN HENNIMAN — 30s, free-lance writer, married to IRIS

WILLIAM REACH — late 20s, a serial killer

## TIME

The present

## PLACE

A maximum security prison. A motel.

# DOWN THE ROAD

## Scene 1

*The set consists of two areas: a motel room with only a double bed and two chairs, and the interview room of a maximum-security prison. In it should be only a table and three chairs. All the chairs should be simple. Other realistic set elements are discouraged. While a tv is heard in the motel at times, and its glow is visible, there should be no tv.*

*Lights up on Dan and Iris in the motel. Day. Iris stands looking out the window. Dan stands across the room, looking at her.*

IRIS.  You all unpacked?

DAN.  Totally and completely. *(She continues to stare out.)* So, feel like taking a walk, or — ?

IRIS.  What's sitting out there? Is that a water heater?

DAN.  Where?

IRIS.  Leaning against that house across the street.

DAN.  Uh, yes — that is a water heater.

IRIS.  It's just sitting there on the front porch.

DAN.  They're probably going to throw it away — it's all rusty.

IRIS.  It's rusty because they're *not* throwing it away. I bet it's been sitting there for years.

DAN.  *(Putting his arms around her from behind.)* Do you consider this a big issue?

IRIS.  *(Moving away from him easily.)* It just caught my eye, that's all. So — you think you're ready?

DAN.  As I'll ever be.

IRIS.  You can't let him get to you. That's the main thing.

7

DAN. I know.
IRIS. We don't want him to clam up. We'd lose the book.
DAN. I *know*. You're not the only one who's interviewed criminals.
IRIS. What criminals have you ever interviewed?
DAN. Those Wall Street guys.
IRIS. Working with you on a crime book. I must be crazy.
DAN. Hey, I'll be great.
IRIS. You will be great, as long as you let me guide you.
DAN. I wish he'd let us interview him together.
IRIS. Maybe he thinks he can shock us more one at a time. But it's better this way. We can set up two psychologies with him — see more sides.
DAN. How come I have to go first?
IRIS. So he'll respect you. If I go first, he'll treat you like the second string.
DAN. Ah.
IRIS. Don't know why I'm trying to sound like such an expert. I've interviewed lots of murderers, but never a serial killer. *(A beat.)* Are you worried about what he'll tell you?
DAN. Of course.
IRIS. Whatever he says, you can't react. If you do —
DAN. I know. He might clam up.
IRIS. Or start playing games. *(Dan turns, looks at her, smiles.)*
DAN. Tell you the only games *I'm* interested in.
IRIS. Dan —
DAN. *(Reaching for her.)* It's the motel. I can never control myself in a motel.
IRIS. Well, learn. We'll be here for months.
DAN. *(All the more inflamed.)* Months!
IRIS. We haven't even walked outside yet. *(He kisses her, moves her to the bed.)* Dan, this isn't professional. *(Lights fade to black.)*

## Scene 2

*Between scenes we hear the voices of Dan and Reach over speakers. Lights rise on Iris in the motel. Evening. She sits on the bed with a small tape recorder, listening. At the same time, the conversation we've been hearing shifts and now emanates from the tape recorder.*

DAN. April second. 11:30 am. First interview with William Reach.

REACH. You're organized.

DAN. You understand that you can in no way profit by the publication of the book we're writing about you? — *Reach isn't doing it for money*

REACH. I understand.

DAN. You have no objection?

REACH. No objection. (*Lights crossfade, shifting from the motel room to the prison interview room. We see Reach and Dan sitting across the table from each other. Reach — who's in handcuffs — wears drab, institutional clothing. On the table is a briefcase and tape recorder. It's the same conversation we've been listening to on the tape, and now their voices take over from the tape.*)

DAN. Bill, we're here to facilitate your book. This is your account, your ... actions. Other books have been written about you, but this is the first to come directly from you. We want to help make this an important and useful document. (*A beat.*) So. Is there anything you want to know about me?

REACH. What's your name again? — *Why ask if he's letting Dan write about him*

DAN. Dan. Dan Henniman.

REACH. Ever write about someone like me, Dan?

DAN. No. But my wife —

REACH. The publisher — Mr. Scanlon — said you write for *Business Week?* — *Belittling Dan w/ his questions.*

DAN. I used to. Now Iris and I —

REACH. I don't mean to criticize. It's just that I want to get the story told. The best way. — *Belittling again*

DAN. Certainly.

REACH. That's why I'm finally talking.

DAN. It's not the appeal?

*Goes from constantly cutting him off to letting Dan speak*

REACH. Sorry?

DAN. You just appealed your sentence of life without parole, right? And your appeal was denied? *— Reach has no hope of getting out*

REACH. Yes, I'm afraid it was.

DAN. So, isn't that the reason you're speaking out now? Since in a sense you have nothing to lose. *(Reach stares at him.)* Sorry, I'm putting words in your mouth.

REACH. That's all right.

DAN. You tell me your reasons if you want to — fair enough? *(Reach nods.)* So. How many people have you killed?

REACH. At least nineteen.

DAN. You don't know the exact number?

REACH. I know it was at least nineteen.

DAN. Are you saying there are others you haven't admitted to? *(Reach is silent.)* Are there others? *(Reach is silent.)* We'll say nineteen then.

REACH. I hope you're not nervous talking to me.

DAN. Not really.

REACH. You're completely safe. Your wife will be, too. Guard's right outside, looking through that little window. He could be in here in a second. *— Puts the possibility of violence*

DAN. Have you ever been violent? In prison, I mean. *in his head*

REACH. No. *— Good behavior in prison*

DAN. Why not?

REACH. It's not so bad here. *(Lights shift to the motel.)*


# Scene 3

*Iris stands looking out the window. Evening. She holds a tape recorder and speaks into it.*


IRIS. Took my first walk yesterday. Gas station, gas station, mini-mart, KFC, quick-stop, gas station, Taco Bell, a worse motel than this one and the Interstate. Dan's out walking right now. The prison's ten miles from here. Twenty miles from anywhere else. *(A beat.)* Dan, you sound fine on these tapes. I think he feels very positive about you. *(A beat.)* I'm feeling pretty positive about you myself tonight. Yesterday was nice. *(Something outside catches her eye again.)* I can*not* stop looking at that water heater. At night there's a yellowish light from the gas station that makes the water heater look almost extraterrestrial. Why do they keep it? Whoever lives there must think of it as — what? Adornment? Why am I looking at it? I'm *not*. *(She looks away. Slowly she looks back out the window. Lights shift to the interview room.)*

## Scene 4

*Dan and Reach are as before.*

DAN. Let's start with Cindy Lauterber. She was the first person you ever ... she was the first, right? — *1st murder*

REACH. Of the nineteen? Yes. *(A beat.)* — *Makes sure he knows its the first of the 19 he admitted*

DAN. She was a stranger.

REACH. Yes.

DAN. How did you ... um, how did you — ?

REACH. Meet her? In a mall. Middle of the day. I called in sick to work.

DAN. *(Consulting his notes.)* To the ... the vending machine company?

REACH. Yeah, I called in sick and —

DAN. You had a route and filled machines, right?

REACH. You know that.

DAN. Yes, sorry. You called in sick?

REACH. I couldn't face it that day, so I went to the mall. Saw this woman — God, how old? She was —

DAN. Eighteen.

REACH. Picked her up.

DAN. How?

REACH. She was pretty. I told her I was a magazine photographer. Asked her to come out to my car so I could take a

11

couple pictures — show my editor.

DAN. And she went?

REACH. They always went.

DAN. She wasn't suspicious?

REACH. Not really.

DAN. Why not?

REACH. I was charming. — *Way of getting women*

DAN. Had you ever done this before?

REACH. Picked up girls with that line? Sure. — *Uses this a lot*

DAN. Had you killed them? Or had you stopped at raping them?

REACH. Dan, I'm really uncomfortable talking about any more victims than nineteen. I hope that's not a problem.

DAN. Cindy and you got to your car. Your camera was in the car? You unlocked the car?

REACH. Right.

DAN. You took your camera out?

REACH. No. It was in the back, on the floor. I pretended it was caught under the seat. You know, the strap. I asked her to slide the seat up. She had to sit in the seat to do that.

DAN. And when she sat in the seat, what did you do?

REACH. Pulled a knife. Grabbed her. Pulled her door shut. Took about two seconds.

DAN. She was yours, then? What did you feel when you took control of somebody like that?

REACH. What did I feel? Relief.

DAN. You had succeeded. ←

REACH. It was by far the best part of it. Always.

DAN. It wasn't killing them?

*Not best part* → REACH. Killing was necessary, but it wasn't ... *(Reach trails off.)*

DAN. Same for the sex? Necessary, but not ... the best?

REACH. You think you know a lot about this.

DAN. No, I only —

REACH. Maybe I should interview you.

DAN. I don't mean —

REACH. Since you're such an expert.

DAN. I'm sorry, all right? *(A beat.)* I really do apologize. What about the mutilation? Was that secondary too? To the control

12

of another human being?

REACH. You mean was control the engine that pulled the train? Yes, it was.

DAN. How would you characterize it? The control. Was it control over women? Society? Life and death? Your mother?

REACH. Does it matter?

DAN. That's not much of an answer.

REACH. It's not much of a question.

DAN. You don't think it's important? Why you did this? (*A beat. Dan sighs.*) All right, we'll write down control over everything. Fair enough?

REACH. I can go with that. (*Lights shift to the motel.*)

## Scene 5

*Iris is as before, speaking into the tape.*

IRIS. I spent the afternoon talking to a prison guard's wife. She says if you're in a prison, you must deserve to be there. Innocent or guilty she says, if you're there, the Good Lord meant you to be. I asked her if she thought that was true for the guards as well. "Especially the guards," she said. "Including your husband?" I asked. "Especially my husband." (*She turns it off as Dan enters from the bathroom.*)

DAN. So, you listened to the tape?

IRIS. Most of it. He sounds like a lot of fun.

DAN. He is. Straining at the seams to convince me he's human. What's scary is, he almost can. The whole time I was trying to make him comfortable — apologizing to a serial killer.

IRIS. He's a source, like anyone else. You're putting him at ease.

DAN. Who's going to put me at ease?

IRIS. I'm actually looking forward to going in tomorrow.

DAN. Yeah, now that I've gone first. Made all the mistakes, cleared the way for the pro.

IRIS. *(Smiling.)* Yeah, thanks. You didn't make any mistakes, though. Not any big ones. He likes you.

DAN. *(Sitting.)* Not sure how to take that.

IRIS. Why are you sitting down? I thought you wanted to go to a movie.

DAN. Oh — right. Forgot.

IRIS. We'll need all the escapism we can get.

DAN. *(Starting to rise tiredly.)* True.

IRIS. You're really not up for this, are you? I know what you need. Lie down on the bed.

DAN. What about the movie?

IRIS. I'll make one. Get on the bed and close your eyes. *(He lies on the bed, face up.)* Roll over. *(He does so. She kneels on the bed, rubs his back.)*

DAN. Ohh, yes ...

IRIS. You feel like you've been beaten with a rope. Are your eyes closed?

DAN. Yes. *(They aren't.)*

IRIS. Good. Tonight's movie is a travelogue.

DAN. A what?

IRIS. Quiet, these used to be quite popular. The title is, *A Map Of What She'll Look Like.*

DAN. That's a travelogue?

IRIS. *(Rubbing him hard.)* Shhh! *(Dan groans deeply.)* A Map Of What She'll Look Like, directed by Iris Henniman. With help from Dan Henniman. We start with her hands. They're tremendously strong. They hold us with the first need. Almost as if it's the earth itself that holds us, not her. We lift her up, and her body works in the air as though she's walking to heaven. Her eyes ... are heaven — the only time we'll see it in our lives.

DAN. That's good.

IRIS. Don't interrupt. She bears us, just as we've borne her. She gives us the world she's come from, and all we can give in return is this one. We owe her everything. We'll never be able to pay. Staring into her face, we realize she looks exactly the way we always dreamed our souls looked. More than innocent. More than pure. Completely untouched. *(As her hands*

14

*range up to the back of his neck and then through his hair.)* Her hair will be exactly like ... mine, I think. But her skin will be yours. The same feel, the same life rising through it — like nothing I've ever felt before. Something I'd never known I'd lost until the moment I found it. *(She starts to kiss the back of his neck. He rolls over, stares up at her.)* We still can, you know. Tonight.

DAN. We can?

IRIS. You still want to go for a girl, don't you? *(He smiles, nods.)* Then let's get started. *(They kiss again, with an easy passion.)*

DAN. Should we be thinking of names while we — ?

IRIS. Shut up. *(They kiss. Lights fade to black.)*

## Scene 6

*Lights fade up again on the motel. Morning. We hear Dan's and Iris's voices from the bathroom.*

DAN. Madeleine.

IRIS. No.

DAN. Hillary.

IRIS. I'm sick of Hillary. Everyone has a Hillary. Hordes of little Hillarys running around.

DAN. Mike.

IRIS. Mike's a boy's name.

DAN. I knew a woman named Mike.

IRIS. *(Entering.)* And a very lucky woman she was, too.

DAN. *(Entering.)* Iris.

IRIS. One's plenty. I had a great time last night.

DAN. Me, too. What if it didn't take?

IRIS. You're right. We'd better do it again immediately.

DAN. Time out! If last night didn't get you pregnant, nothing's going to.

IRIS. We have to do it a lot at certain times —

DAN. I understand; we'll get a girl. *(Handing her the briefcase.)*

You going to be all right with him?
IRIS. You're still in one piece. *(She kisses him, moves to go.)*
DAN. Don't let him get to you.
IRIS. I think I'm pregnant. 'Bye. *(Dan smiles. She exits. Lights shift to interview room.)*


## Scene 7

*Reach sits with Iris, reading her something he's written.*

REACH. "Hi, lover. Bet you wondered why I've been so late writing back. Must be 'cause I'm writing all my other girls. Ha. Just kidding. How are things in Mobile? I think of you all the time, the way you are in that picture you sent. You know the one I mean. It's my connection with you. Connections are so important. You like the one I sent of me? I was in college then, but I still look the same. Same great looks. Ha. I think we were meant to meet and hold hands together, no matter how far away we might be. Holding hands in a world of uncertain destinies. All my love ..." What do you think?
IRIS. Who is she?
REACH. Just a fan. You like my style?
IRIS. It's ... conversational. Can we have a copy?
REACH. *(Handing letter and photo to her.)* Go ahead; use it. *(Iris puts them into her briefcase.)* You know, I've read all your books. Scanlon sent them to me. You're very good.
IRIS. Thanks.
REACH. You never have a picture on the jacket. *(A beat.)* You're younger than I thought. Prettier.
IRIS. *(Turning on the tape recorder.)* So are you. Tell me, Bill — when you had sex with Cindy Lauterber, was she alive or dead? *(A beat.)* We're not quite sure from yesterday's tape, that's all. *(A beat.)* We really do depend on you for accuracy. *(A beat.)* Do you have trouble talking about the sexual part of it? *(A beat.)* Why do you think you have trouble talking about that?

REACH. I don't like why questions.
IRIS. Why not?
REACH. Ask me a how question.
IRIS. How come you don't like why questions? *(He looks off disgustedly.)* How did you kill Cindy?
REACH. With a knife.
IRIS. And you did this right away, or — ?
REACH. I drove her to the lake first.
IRIS. Sugar Lake?
REACH. That's right.
IRIS. How many bodies did you leave in the hills near Sugar Lake?
REACH. Nine. No — ten.
IRIS. Once you and Cindy got there, did you kill her in the car, or — ?
REACH. I made her get out. She yelled. No one was around.
IRIS. Did she try to run?
REACH. I had hold of her. Are you afraid of me?
IRIS. Desperately. What happened next?
REACH. She tried talking. I told her to shut up.
IRIS. Were you afraid you'd get to know her? *(A beat.)* When did you stab her?
REACH. Right then.
IRIS. How many times?
REACH. Seven, eight — I don't know. She fought. I was nervous. I cut myself. Finally she went unconscious. She made a sound, and ... my arm was bleeding.
IRIS. Is that when you raped her?
REACH. Is it rape if they're dead?
IRIS. So she was dead?
REACH. When I finished, I threw her down the hill.
IRIS. Didn't bury her?
REACH. No, the ... animals. You know. Then I bandaged myself, drove home.
IRIS. How did you feel? As you drove.
REACH. Scared. Perfect.
IRIS. Perfect?
REACH. Like God. *(Lights shift to the motel.)*

17

## Scene 8

*Day. Dan sits in a chair talking into a tape recorder.*

DAN.  Walked to McDonald's this morning. Car dealer, gas station, Dairy Queen, gas station, tire store, muffler shop, gas station, McDonald's. Incredible landscape. They should get honest and call these strips theme parks: "Oblivion World." Step right up and disappear. *(He turns off the tape, turns it on again.)* Actually, I've walked to McDonald's almost every day for the last two weeks. Pretty easy to get into a rut here. *(A beat.)* Um, Iris? Speaking of ruts, I notice you've been including lots of notes about water heaters. I know it's one of those well-observed details we're always looking for, but you have ... golly, six or seven entries here, and maybe that's enough? *(He turns off the tape, turns it on again.)* I finished rereading the background material on Reach. Every book, newspaper article, magazine spread, talk-show tape, etc., etc. Even reread the t-shirt. Never felt so paranoid in my life. I'm sure this feeling will fade, at some point. *(Staring out the window.)* That water heater's just red with rust. *(Lights fade quickly to black.)*

## Scene 9

*Lights rise on interview room. Reach and Iris are as before.*

IRIS.  Cindy's body —
REACH.  Who?
IRIS.  Cindy. *(Suddenly catching herself.)* Oh — I'm sorry. I got them confused. Paula. Paula's body.
REACH.  Cindy was a couple weeks ago. We're on number five. You need a break?
IRIS.  No, no. Just sometimes they ... run together. *Paula's* body — in fact, all ten of the bodies you left at Sugar Lake — weren't found for years. The remains were fragmentary.

REACH. So?

IRIS. I'm just trying to examine your patterns. Through the first several.... We know you used a knife on some of them. But not always?

REACH. I hit some of them with a rock. Strangled — you know. Sometimes it was kind of messy. I got angry with myself.

IRIS. For killing them ... so badly?

REACH. I got smoother as I went on.

IRIS. Did you ever torture a victim?

REACH. No, I liked being quick.

IRIS. Why?

REACH. I don't know why. That's your job.

IRIS. This is your book, Bill. I can't speculate about your motives. So. Why did you like to be quick?

REACH. Most people don't torture what they hunt. *(A beat.)*

IRIS. Fair enough. What was it like choosing someone?

REACH. Moving targets. I'd stand around — mall, carnival, bar. I don't know what I was looking for. The way someone looked. Or if she acted tentative. If I smiled and she smiled back. Even just her clothes.

IRIS. Skimpy clothes? Expensive?

REACH. Just nice. Nice, clean look. Done up, not careless. I'd see a girl like that and want her.

IRIS. Why didn't you just have her?

REACH. What?

IRIS. You were single, good-looking. You probably could've gone to bed with a lot of these women.

REACH. Sure, but what's the point? That wouldn't've been different from what anybody else does. *(A beat.)*

IRIS. Let's take a different angle. Paula Milstrom —

REACH. Number five.

IRIS. Right, I'm with it now. You met Paula in a bar and took her home. You were living alone at that time. You had sex with her? *(He nods.)* In a more or less normal — ?

REACH. Yeah.

IRIS. And afterwards, when she was asleep — ?

REACH. I stabbed her.

IRIS. Why? *(He's silent.)* You kept her in the apartment, right? After you'd killed her. For how long? Six days, is that right? Before you brought her body to Sugar Lake?
REACH. Yeah.
IRIS. You just kept her there. Why?
REACH. I liked her. *(Lights fade quickly to black.)*


## Scene 10

*Instantly we hear a woman's scream: long, terrified — very disturbing. A beat. The woman screams again. Another very short beat, then a hesitant smattering of applause that quickly builds to a crescendo and then dies down. During the applause lights fade up in the motel room to reveal Dan watching tv. It's night. We hear the voice of a Talk-Show Host.*

HOST. Well, well, *well.* So what's this picture called again? *Bambi Meets Godzilla?*
MALE GUEST. *(With a laugh.)* You could call it that.
HOST. No, you play a killer.
MALE GUEST. A serial killer.
HOST. Right. There's more of that these days, isn't there?
MALE GUEST. Lots more.
HOST. Gruesome thought. Who does your guy kill?
MALE GUEST. Very beautiful women. Cover girls only: *Vogue, Elle, Cosmopolitan —*
HOST. *Sports Illustrated. (Mild audience laughter.)* That's what we think of with *Sports Illustrated* nowadays, isn't it?
MALE GUEST. Depends on what you call sports.
HOST. I know what *I* call sports. *(Big audience laugh. Dan rises and moves toward the glow. He gestures and the tv turns off.)*
DAN. We got a call from Scanlon. Iris?
IRIS. *(Calling from the bathroom.)* What?
DAN. Scanlon called.
IRIS. *(Entering from the bathroom.)* What did he want?

DAN. Wanted to know how it was going. Told him it was going fine, we're marching through the first several of the famous nineteen murders —

IRIS. If there were only nineteen.

DAN. And that Reach was cooperative, informative and graphic when pressed.

IRIS. What did Scanlon say?

DAN. He wanted to know how graphic.

IRIS. Publishers.

DAN. What's he want us to do? Hype the gore?

IRIS. It hypes itself. *(Moving to the bed, sitting.)* I've interviewed men who murdered their friends, their wives, eight people in a City Hall. No one like him.

DAN. Scanlon also wanted to know how the other side of it was going. The note file. Our impressions.

IRIS. What did you say?

DAN. Said it was going great. Hopeless town, empty lives, wilderness that's practically Biblical.

IRIS. Good. *(She starts for the bathroom again.)*

DAN. Didn't say a word about this. *(Dan turns on the tape recorder. We hear Iris's voice.)*

IRIS. *(On tape.)* There's a woman sitting next to the water heater. Middle-aged, shapeless house-dress. She's wearing sunglasses, staring east. I believe she serves the water heater in some way. Perhaps she's the high priestess, I'm not sure.

DAN. *(Turning it off.)* What am I listening to?

IRIS. Nothing. I was just kidding around. *(Dan fast-forwards the tape, turns it on again. Iris on tape.)* Able-bodied men walk in and out of the house. These are obviously her slaves. She or the water heater itself exerts a highly-sophisticated form of mind-control —

DAN. *(Turning it off.)* Whole paragraphs of "kidding around"?

IRIS. It's an impression. We agreed to record our impressions.

DAN. Our impressions, not our fixations.

IRIS. If you have a problem with this, say so. Don't pull a grand inquisitor routine with the tape.

DAN. I thought things were going fine.

IRIS. They are.

DAN. Is this something you always do when you're interviewing? Does it break the tension, or —
IRIS. I happened to see a water heater, get fascinated, record a lot of silliness — ok?! It was a lapse.
DAN. What kind of lapse?
IRIS. *Dan* —
DAN. I'm trying to learn, that's all. Why a water heater?
IRIS. What else is there!? There's an Interstate and a water heater — that's it! Oh, and at the prison we get to spend half our time with the sickest man on the planet. What do you want me to fixate on?
DAN. I still don't see why you have to make a novella out of a water heater.
IRIS. *Is this just a style-point, or what!? (A beat. She sits in a chair. As she does so, lights come up faintly on the interview room. Reach is sitting there.)* With most murderers it's, "I hated this, I hated that, I hated everything." With Reach, it's just ... a wall. "Why did you kill her?".
REACH. I don't know.
IRIS. "How did you kill her?".
REACH. Stabbed her ten times. Strangled her with a nylon rope, nearly severed her head from her body.
IRIS. "What did you do then?".
REACH. Raped her.
IRIS. "Then what?".
REACH. Cut her head off, took it home, set it on a table, stared at it.
IRIS. "Then what?".
REACH. Had sex with it.
IRIS. "And how did you feel?".
REACH. What?
IRIS. "When you did that, how did you feel?". *(Reach hesitates, shrugs.)* He could have been stripping a chair. *(Lights fade out on the interview room.)* I thought nothing could bother me — that I could listen to the most horrible things. *(Lights crossfade to the interview room. As they do so, Dan simply crosses from the motel room to the interview room with his briefcase. Reach is still sitting there.)*

# Scene 11

*Reach is reading Dan a letter Reach has received.*

REACH. "... no one who looks like you, and talks like you, could do what they say you have done. It's not possible, and even if it was, God would forgive it. You are obviously a man of worth and not trash like some. You have a rare quality of charm not even the man on *Sixty Minutes* can refuse. I hope you don't think I'm forward to send my picture ..." *(Reach pulls a snapshot out of his pocket and hands it to Dan.)* "... but since I know what you look like, I thought it could make us equal in a small way. All my prayers and love ..." And then she signs her name.

DAN. Can I see that?

REACH. *(Giving Dan the letter.)* Enjoy yourself. I've got plenty of 'em. *(Dan stares from letter to picture.)* She's cute.

DAN. What? Oh.... Let's get to work. *(Dan puts the letter and photo in the briefcase.)*

REACH. What about the title?

DAN. What?

REACH. Of the book. Scanlon keeps giving me the runaround. Won't give a firm yes to any of the titles I've suggested.

DAN. You're talking titles with him?

REACH. I like *First Blood*, but he said it was a movie.

DAN. It was.

REACH. He didn't like *Blood Trail*, either. Sounded like a Western.

DAN. Well —

REACH. He thought *Blood Fury*, but I don't know.

DAN. Maybe Iris and I should give Scanlon a call and suggest some of our own.

REACH. If you think it'll help.

DAN. *(Turning on the tape.)* April 30th. 11:30 am. Bill, today I'd like you to talk about the death of Melanie Bryce.

REACH. Great.

DAN. She was your, um ... *(Looking at his notes.)* Your ninth victim, right?

REACH. About that, yeah.

DAN. This one involved a trip of some days, isn't that right?

REACH. Six days.

DAN. You were in another state.

REACH. I took a few days off.

DAN. Did the vending company know where you were?

REACH. No.

DAN. You didn't tell them you were leaving.

REACH. The machines would be there when I got back.

DAN. You didn't tell your fiancee, either?

REACH. She was never my fiancee. We never set a date.

DAN. I thought she was.

REACH. I gave her a ring, that's all. I'd practically left her by then anyway.

DAN. I thought she left you.

REACH. I thought we were talking about Melanie Bryce.

DAN. Did you often leave for days at a time?

REACH. Yeah.

DAN. And your ... um, Donna never got worried or suspicious?

REACH. She got puzzled. I told her not to be. Told her I needed time to be alone. Men need that, don't they?

DAN. You met Melanie Bryce — she was sixteen? — in, um —

REACH. Edwardsville.

DAN. Three hundred miles from your home. You picked her and a friend up near their high school.

REACH. It was raining. Real downpour. They stuck their thumbs out.

DAN. Her friend was Gina Miller.

REACH. Guess so. I dropped her off at her house.

DAN. Why?

REACH. Why what?

DAN. Why didn't you kill them both? Later you killed two at a time. Weren't you sure you could handle it, or — ?

REACH. I could handle it.

DAN. But you dropped Gina off. *(A beat.)*
REACH. She wasn't right. She looked — I don't know — she looked unimportant. Messy.
DAN. Ugly?
REACH. No. She was pretty enough.
DAN. Just badly dressed.
REACH. She wasn't right.
DAN. So. You were alone with Melanie. What happened?
REACH. I pulled a gun right away. Made her bend down out of sight. Had her put her hands behind her back. Taped her hands, taped her mouth.
DAN. As you drove?
REACH. While we were stopped at a light. Then I took her down the road.
DAN. Where?
REACH. Sugar Lake.
DAN. But before that?
REACH. An empty farmhouse I knew about.
DAN. *(Looking at notes.)* This was the farm owned by —
REACH. Don't know.
DAN. John Berthelsen, about thirty miles from your home.
REACH. Right.
DAN. So you drove Melanie two hundred seventy miles while she was alive and conscious? What did you talk about?
REACH. Her mouth was taped.
DAN. Sorry.
REACH. Don't you listen?
DAN. Did you talk to her?
REACH. Asked if she was comfortable.
DAN. You got her in the farmhouse, you ... broke in? You ... did she struggle?
REACH. No. She was pretty tired, cramped from how she was sitting.
DAN. You entered the farmhouse. You took her where? The bedroom?
REACH. The kitchen.
DAN. Why?
REACH. There was a sink. *(A beat.)*

DAN. Did you kill her right away?

REACH. No, I tied her in a chair.

DAN. Did you have sex? At that point?

REACH. At that point. At that point. That's all you guys want to hear about, isn't it? Yeah, orally.

DAN. You mean you — ?

REACH. She blew me. I made her do that.

DAN. Did you have an orgasm?

REACH. What's wrong with you?

DAN. Nothing —

REACH. Are you getting excited?

DAN. No, Bill, I'm not getting excited. I'm asking you questions for the book.

REACH. Well, if you're not getting excited, who is?

DAN. Hopefully, no one.

REACH. Uh-huh. And this is a scholarly publication we're working on, isn't it?

DAN. Are you ashamed you had an orgasm, or ashamed you didn't?

REACH. I came in her mouth and killed her. Bim-bam. Next question.

DAN. How did you — ?

REACH. Slit her throat with my fishing knife.

DAN. That's a lot of blood. Weren't you afraid — ?

REACH. I know how not to leave clues.

DAN. You cut her head off. Did you do that then?

REACH. Yes. Put it in a plastic bag, threw it in the trunk of my car.

DAN. The body?

REACH. Garbage bag. Threw it in the trunk. Washed up the kitchen, got in my car and — zip.

DAN. To Sugar Lake. The dumping ground. You tossed the body, and ... took the head home?

REACH. Not directly. I had to stop and see my therapist. The guy the court assigned me.

DAN. After your rape conviction?

REACH. It wasn't rape. I bargained that down to third-degree. Never served any time for that. So I had my last session with the therapist that day.

DAN. And you drove there, with Melanie Bryce's head in your car's trunk, and had your last session with him?

REACH. That's right.

DAN. What did he say to you, that last day?

REACH. He said he thought I'd made real progress. *(Lights fade to black.)*

## Scene 12

*Lights rise on the motel. Day. Iris sits with some papers in her lap. We hear the sound of a radio news report.*

ANNOUNCER. The bodies of the two girls were found at the bottom of an abandoned well, in a wooded area. Their uncle led authorities to the site as part of an agreement which will allow him to be charged with two counts of second-degree murder only —

IRIS. Christ.

ANNOUNCER. A spokesman for the county attorney's office expressed regret that this was the only way to discover the victims' remains. The children's parents —

IRIS. *(Rising, moving towards the tv.)* Christ.

ANNOUNCER. ... when asked how they felt, said this: *(Iris makes a gesture. Radio falls silent.)*

IRIS. Must be why they put the radio in the tv — you can't throw it out the window. *(We hear Dan's voice from the street.)*

DAN. *(Off.)* Iris? Iris? *(He enters.)* Good — you're here.

IRIS. How was your day?

DAN. Fabulous. I vomited in the parking lot.

IRIS. Oh.

DAN. You would not believe what that man's done.

IRIS. I know what he's done. *(Dan exits directly into the bathroom.)*

DAN. *(Off. Over the sound of running water.)* To know is not to hear him say it.

IRIS. I've heard him say a lot of things.

DAN. *(Off.)* You did not hear Melanie Bryce. *(At this point Reach — not Dan — enters from the bathroom. Reach does not seem visible to Iris, though he smiles shyly at her. He's still in handcuffs. Reach moves to the window and looks out. Iris continues talking to Dan.)*

IRIS. Must've been pretty bad.

DAN. *(Off.)* Pretty bad. *(Reentering from the bathroom.)* Come on, we're going out to eat.

IRIS. You're hungry?

DAN. I have an empty stomach, remember? Besides, we'll be driving a long time.

IRIS. How come?

DAN. Because we're not stopping till we get to a four-star restaurant.

IRIS. There isn't one in the state.

DAN. So what?

IRIS. So how far do you intend to go? All the way back to New York?

DAN. Why not?

IRIS. Are you serious?

DAN. I could give it up, if you could. Honest, today I could.

IRIS. I know how you feel. Come here, give me a hug.

DAN. A hug doesn't speak to the —

IRIS. Give me a hug. I'm pregnant.

DAN. You're what?

IRIS. Congratulations. You've just uttered the most inevitable line in the history of conversation. "You're what?". I'm pregnant. Now you say:

DAN. That's wonderful.

IRIS. And I say, "Isn't it?!". And we hug. Hug me. *(Dan does so.)* And then I say, "Aside from the fact that we'd never work for Scanlon again, and lose all our credibility in the business, *and* run away from something we've started — there is now this. We can't quit our day job. Not now. *(Dan sighs, releases her. He sits in a chair. Reach — still apparently not visible to either Dan or Iris, turns and watches them.)*

DAN. What are we doing here?

IRIS. What do you mean?

DAN. With Reach. Maybe there are some kinds of murderers.... Well, you've said it yourself — sometimes you're embarrassed to walk by the "True Crime" shelf in a bookstore. You wonder, "Who *is* that reading my book? Why are they interested?"

IRIS. Dan —

DAN. Why *are* they interested?

IRIS. If we leave this project, Scanlon will go out and get someone who can listen to Bill Reach. He won't have to look very far. The book will get written and published. Inevitably.

DAN. As inevitably as those girls got murdered?

IRIS. We can make sure the job is accurate, and as objective as possible. If we leave — *(Dan sighs resignedly.)* How about if we just try to get through the next group? After Melanie Bryce they won't seem so bad. When that's done, we can change subjects with him for awhile. Do background stuff: school, childhood. I've been getting more interested in that angle anyway.

DAN. I don't know what it is. I feel ... abandoned out here. I feel like we're out in the open.

IRIS. We're not abandoned, we're together. Ok? *(She kisses his cheek, rises, moves toward the bathroom.)*

DAN. Is it a girl?

IRIS. If there's any hope in science. *(She exits into the bathroom. After a moment, Reach rises and surveys the room. Dan hasn't moved and doesn't seem to see Reach.)*

REACH. Must be hard to sleep in a room like this. Right off the highway. Must be loud. You have a good marriage? Motel life'll kill any relationship, that's my experience. I've stayed in this chain. Rooms are terrible. Closets never have enough hangers, bathmats feel like they're alive. And that view of yours. I worried when I heard this was where you were staying. It's not good enough. Not if you're working with me. *(Reach kneels down a few feet in front of Dan.)* Does your wife still excite you? *(Dan shifts his gaze to Reach. Lights crossfade to interview room as Reach turns and moves directly there.)*

# Scene 13

*Reach sits. Iris turns on the tape.*

IRIS. Bill, I know we planned to talk about victims today, but instead I'd like to go into some of your background.

REACH. How come?

IRIS. Change of pace. I want to ask you about college today. Dan will cover your childhood later.

REACH. I had a bad childhood. My mother was married three times.

IRIS. Dan'll ask about that. Let's see — you went into college straight from high school, right? Then took your BA in four years?

REACH. Yeah.

IRIS. You changed majors a few times. Any reason?

REACH. I liked it all. I was a good student.

IRIS. You settled on English — not the most practical, I can tell you. Then you got into a master's program in business management, right?

REACH. That's right.

IRIS. You were in this program a little more than a year and a half. Then suddenly you quit. With — what? — one quarter to go? Why?

REACH. I don't know why. I was already ... *(Trails off.)*

IRIS. You were already raping women.

REACH. Yeah.

IRIS. Still, nobody knew that. Not at the time. Why didn't you finish? Were you out of money, or — ?

REACH. I was a criminal.

IRIS. You weren't picked up till the following fall. Did you actually say, "I'm raping women now, I'll have to stop school"? *(He stares at her.)* Sorry, is this making you uncomfortable? I'm just trying to give you the chance to say in your own words why you did certain things. *(He stares at her.)* Let's go on to something during the killings.

REACH. Fine.

IRIS. You had a lot of jobs, right? The vending machine job, then you quit that and picked up a job in telephone sales — why?

REACH. I could make my own hours.

IRIS. But just a few months later you left to clerk in a sporting goods store.

REACH. What's wrong with that?

IRIS. All these jobs just seem so unambitious. You nearly had a Master's degree. *(A beat.)* A year after that you went to work for an advertising firm, but you were really little more than a gofer.

REACH. They said I'd move up.

IRIS. But you didn't.

REACH. *(With sudden force.)* I'm not here to talk about jobs! *(A sharp rapping — sound of a nightstick on the metal door. They both look towards the door. Iris waves, calls out.)*

IRIS. Everything's fine. *(Reach relaxes somewhat, smiles and waves at the door. His smile disappears when he looks at her.)*

REACH. I kill women, you know.

IRIS. Not anymore. *(A beat.)*

REACH. I changed jobs because of the killings. I didn't want people I worked with getting suspicious.

IRIS. You never changed where you lived. What about your neighbors?

REACH. What's going on here? Why are you harping on this?

IRIS. I'm just puzzled —

REACH. There's nothing puzzling. *Nothing puzzling.* Understand? *(A beat.)* Does Scanlon know you're asking me a bunch of irrelevant questions? Do you want me to call him?

IRIS. No, I don't want you to call him, Bill. I'm sorry if I've offended you.

REACH. We're through talking about jobs.

IRIS. All right. I honestly do apologize if I hit a nerve.

REACH. You didn't hit a nerve. Move on to something else.

IRIS. Sure, um ... I really do want to cover things in this period. Ok, let's talk about your fiancee.

REACH. She was not my fiancee.

.S.   I thought she was.
EACH.   *I only gave her a ring! (Lights shift to the motel.)*

## Scene 14

*Day. Dan stares out the window, talks into the tape recorder.*

DAN.   I talk to Bill about his childhood tomorrow — taking a vacation from his ... road trips. The scariest thing is that his upbringing wasn't scary. Couple stepfathers, but no abuse, beatings, molestation. Only child — so are millions. In a juvenile center for awhile — so are thousands. Didn't like his mother much, but she was no monster. His home life was marked by what you'd have to call — in this country at least — the usual emptiness. *(Dan rises, goes closer to the window.)* I've started dreaming about the Interstate. Mile after mile, every night. Utterly familiar by now, but ... featureless. Where's it come from? Everywhere. Where's it go? Everywhere. The other day, driving to work, I caught myself fantasizing about just going on: ignoring the exit, following the next bend in the highway, the next. Getting lost on the largest engineering project in the history of the world. Floating there. No set destination, no limit to where you go. Parallel universe. If someone wants a ride ... give 'em a ride. Nothing matters. Newspaper, tv, radio — it's their state, not yours; their problem, not yours; their daughter, not — *(Dan shuts off the tape, rewinds it briefly, plays it back to "... their problem, not yours ..." and stops it there. He starts recording again.)* In the decade of the 1950's, before completion of the Interstate, there was only one case of serial murder reported in the United States. In the whole decade, just one. Now — one a month. *(Lights shift back to the interview room.)*

# Scene 15

*Iris and Reach are as before.*

IRIS. So. Donna was your girlfriend, not your fiancee. Her father owned a successful trucking firm. Ever think of going into that?

REACH. They wanted me to.

IRIS. Were you interested?

REACH. It could've been a lot of money, but —

IRIS. But what?

REACH. We're talking about jobs again.

IRIS. Oh, I'm sorry. Let's —

REACH. I'm definitely calling Scanlon.

IRIS. That's your right. I hope you don't. Donna and you broke up — for the first time, anyway — not long before you killed your first victim, Cindy Lauterber. Is that right?

REACH. So?

IRIS. Some people theorize that the trigger for the first time you went beyond rape and killed was Donna's rejection of you.

REACH. Who thinks that?

IRIS. A number of people. Is it wrong?

REACH. A.) She did not reject me; I rejected her. B.) Only after I rejected her did she reject me. C.) After we rejected each other, she crawled back to me and not vice-versa. And this happened several times.

IRIS. So it has no relationship to any of these crimes?

REACH. Why should it? She was just my girlfriend.

IRIS. You had a college degree — could've had a Master's. Career opportunities if you wanted them, a relationship with a woman — whom you loved?

REACH. I loved her.

IRIS. Yet essentially you rejected every chance to succeed. Why? *(A beat.)* What do you think of the theory that your killings were the acts of a man who hadn't formed a complete identity? A man who needed to kill people in order to be anyone at all. *(Reach is silent.)* Do you agree with that?

ACH. Who are you?

IS. Iris Henniman.

REACH. And in a hundred years, who are you going to be?

IRIS. Dead — that's who I'm going to be.

REACH. That's right. But I'll still be William Reach. Why do you think you're not writing about the guy who killed his family anymore? Or the guy who went berserk with his M-16? Don't talk to me about identities. You've got a chance — just a chance — to be somebody here. Stick to what Scanlon pays you for.

IRIS. What Scanlon pays me for —

REACH. What Scanlon pays you for is to write my book! Mine! Why doesn't matter. I did it — other men didn't. Besides, your theory is shit. I killed someone before Cindy Lauterber. She wasn't the first.

IRIS. Who else did you kill? *(Reach is silent.)* How do I know you're not just trying to undermine these theories? *(Reach is silent.)* The victim's family would like to know. *(Reach is silent.)* It should be in the book. If we're collaborators —

REACH. *It's for the sequel, bitch! (Sharp rapping on the door, which continues as lights fade to black.)*

## Scene 16

*In the darkness, we hear the sound of a Donohuesque Talk-Show Host on the motel tv. The tv's glow rises, followed by lights on the motel. Watching tv are Dan and Reach. Dan's on the edge of the bed, Reach sits on the floor.*

HOST.   ... but how do we recognize them? What do we know about them? What do they want? Is it only to kill? Is it sex? Is it sex *and* killing? Doctor? *(We hear the monotone of an expert guest.)*

GUEST. It's hard to say. Mass slayers often want sex, but the killing is what gives them the real sense of satisfaction.

HOST. A very distorted sense.

GUEST. But maybe the only real satisfaction they can achie
*(Iris enters from the street. She carries the briefcase.)*
IRIS. Hi.
HOST. How do we identify them? That's what's really important here, isn't it?
IRIS. What's this?
DAN. They're doing serial killers.
HOST. We can theorize all we want, but how can I tell, walking down the street, who's going to kill me and who's not?
IRIS. Oh, great.
GUEST. I don't think you can —
HOST. I've got to! It's life or death! One clue — anyone. *(Iris moves to the tv.)* Any of our guests. Some of you have been attacked. What did you notice? What do these men have in common? *(She turns the sound off. The glow remains.)*
REACH. Hey. *(Iris ignores Reach, who keeps watching the tv.)*
IRIS. *(To Dan.)* Hope you don't mind.
DAN. Are you kidding? That guy asks three hundred questions in twenty-two minutes, doesn't get an answer to one. "People being slaughtered like cattle? Who cares? Am I still on?" Keeps asking what men like Bill Reach want.
IRIS. To be him; that's what they want.
DAN. *(His arm going around her waist.)* It is, eh? It's not what I want.
IRIS. What do you want?
DAN. *(Suddenly pulling her down on the bed with him.)* I want to talk baby names!
IRIS. Dan — !
DAN. *(Kissing her.)* I thought of many valuable new baby names today. Can't wait to try them out on you.
IRIS. Such as?
DAN. Bitzy.
IRIS. Bitzy?
DAN. It'll be cute. She'll be little —
IRIS. Dan.
DAN. Ok, ok — how about Chloe?
IRIS. *Dan —*
DAN. Give it a chance, it grows on you.

3.   Chloe will never grow on me.
N.   Scarlet? Hildegarde? Fawn?
RIS.   Are these old girlfriends?
DAN.   How about Rachel?
IRIS.   Rachel. That's a possibility. What's it mean?
DAN.   Um ... patient in suffering.
IRIS.   *(Rising, crossing to the window.)* Maybe not.
DAN.   So. How was your day?
IRIS.   Actually, I think I found something out.
DAN.   What?
IRIS.   Something about Reach. His jobs, school record — even Donna. It all really haunted him. He didn't want to talk about any of it. He seemed afraid of what he might say. I think it could be the pivotal issue in his life.
DAN.   School?
IRIS.   Failure.
DAN.   He wasn't a failure. He was an educated, middle-class person.
IRIS.   Not in his eyes. He thought he was nobody.
DAN.   Why would he think that?
IRIS.   Because he was nobody special. Look at the jobs he had: all beneath him. That's no accident.
DAN.   I don't know.
IRIS.   What about this? He hasn't shown the slightest regret over killing and mutilating people, right? But he's utterly ashamed his girlfriend dropped him, he never had a real career, he quit school —
DAN.   He quit grad school.
IRIS.   He quit. At all. At any point. Somewhere along the line Reach got the idea that unless you succeed — *really* succeed, become famous — you don't exist. Don't you see? It explains his choice of victim. Young, middle-class women. For him they weren't even real — just society's prizes. He grabs the prize, kills her, and has his revenge. On society, not on her.
REACH.   *(Quietly, to himself.)* Bullshit.
DAN.   And that's why he rejected killing Gina Miller? She was too poor? Didn't represent the right social group?
IRIS.   Exactly.

REACH. *(Suddenly standing.)* Bullshit! *(Reach strides into the in*
*view room. They pay no attention to him. Lights don't shift with him*
IRIS. Before he started killing women, there was no Bil
Reach. There was, "Hey, you." There was, "Hurry up on your
route today." "You don't understand me," from his lover and,
"You'll get a business degree like fifty thousand other people."
Each day he felt a little more of himself step into an empti-
ness that someone else might not even notice, but that to him
was so complete, so inescapable, that the only way out — the
only way not to be dead himself — was to become a monster.
DAN. Does this really make sense, though? He kills women
'cause he doesn't think he's a success? By that criterion, almost
anyone could become Bill Reach.
IRIS. Maybe anyone could.
DAN. He kills women out of sexual anger.
IRIS. Men rape out of sexual anger. They abuse. They don't
do what Reach does.
DAN. How do you know? How does anyone know how deep
that goes?
IRIS. How do you?
DAN. One thing I do know: if this bothers Reach as much
as you say, there's no way we'll get it in the book.
IRIS. Why not? We can phrase things, shade them —
DAN. How? Between Reach and Scanlon? We can't even get
our own title. We can't prove this theory. So where's that leave
us? We're here to write down what Reach did. In his own
words. That's it, that's our brief: report it. Make it vivid, com-
pelling —
IRIS. Stupid —
DAN. Whatever. It's not for us to decide. Our job's to be a
good pair of journalists. Write the book, get the money, get
another book —
IRIS. And another book, and another —
DAN. And support ourselves. There's nothing wrong with that.
IRIS. Iris and Dan Henniman — crime-writing couple.
DAN. Exactly.
IRIS. Watching our names grow on the covers: first half the
size of the title, then the same size, twice the —

N. It's a business. It's marketing.
S. Henniman crimes! Henniman criminals — better than
her criminals, grislier —
DAN. *Iris* —
IRIS. Somewhere, somehow Bill Reach — a man with no iden-
tity, but a real gift for the twentieth century — found a goal:
to become unforgettable, at any price. Because *something*
taught him that nothing else matters. Don't you want to
know what that something is?
DAN. It's not our job. *(A silence.)* What kind of shape did all
this leave Reach in?
IRIS. A little ruffled.
DAN. How ruffled?
IRIS. It got to him — I said. Even made him a little desper-
ate to disprove it. He claimed he'd killed someone before
Cindy Lauterber.
DAN. Who?
IRIS. He wouldn't say. I don't even think it's true.
DAN. Was it one? Two?
IRIS. It?
DAN. The victim. How many?
IRIS. I think it's just a lie.
DAN. But if it isn't?
IRIS. If it isn't, he's saving it for a sequel.
DAN. He said that?
IRIS. He said that. *(Dan moves into the interview room. Lights shift
with him.)*


## Scene 17

*Dan sets up the tape in the interview room as Reach watches.*

DAN. How are you doing today?
REACH. Fine.
DAN. Nothing bothering you?
REACH. Nope.

DAN. Good. That's good. *(Dan turns on the tape.)* May seve.
11:30 am. Bill, I was going to start with some childhood r
ollections today, but — *(Reach suddenly turns off the tape. I*
*stares at Dan, then turns the tape back on.)*
REACH. May seventh. Today we're going to listen to Bill
Reach for once, instead of all this crap!
DAN. Bill —
REACH. We're going to *listen*. *(Dan is silent.)* No more ques-
tions about college or childhood or jobs or — *No more*. What
I did can't be explained. People don't want explanations
anyway — they just want to know how it felt.
DAN. How did it feel before Cindy Lauterber?
REACH. What?
DAN. With your first victim. Your real first one.
REACH. You think you're being funny?
DAN. I'm only —
REACH. *We talk about what I want to talk about — understand!?*
*(Sharp rapping on the door. Dan waves calmly. Reach rubs his*
*temples.)* You want to know how it feels? I'll tell you. It feels
like ... the middle of space. Floating. Alone. Driving late at
night on a deserted road. Headed directly into a perfect dark
that somehow gets darker. And the road and woods and sky
all roll up together into a huge gateway that's always opening
— just opening as you get there. The feeling of the steering
wheel and the dashboard is so familiar, so ... owned by you.
The girl — the victim — is in the seat beside you. And you're
more alone than if she wasn't there. You understand? *(A beat.)*
A lot of guys would try to deny this. But I feel we can be
honest here, don't you? *(A beat.)* That victim owes you her
breath. It's not hers anymore — from the time she trusted
you. From the time she failed to protect herself. If you don't
want her to breathe, if it gets to you, at any point — what do
you do? Dan?
DAN. You kill her.
REACH. That's logic. Then you get out of the car, and stand
there on the road, in the absolute dark. And you feel a silence, a stillness, that sounds better to you than any human
voice you've ever heard. You can't even remember your own

— or that you ever had one. Then you think about that
~y, and the clothes still on it, and her bag on the floor of
~e car, and the things in that bag — and you decide what
~ou want to keep, and what you want to throw away. *(A beat.)*
You open the car door — the only light's the little courtesy
light in the door — and you go through that bag, and
through those clothes and through that body. And anything
you want is yours. *(A beat.)* You print that. That's what they
want to read. *(Reach turns off the tape. Dan rises, puts the tape into
the briefcase and moves into the motel. Lights shift with him.)*

## Scene 18

*Iris sits looking out the window as Dan enters.*

IRIS. Why are you back so early?
DAN. I'm all done for today. Bill said so.
IRIS. He what?
DAN. He generously provided me with a glimpse into yet a
lower circle of hell, then informed me we were through. Till
tomorrow, anyway. You he doesn't want to see ever again.
IRIS. That's impossible.
DAN. You were right when you said you ruffled him. Today
he was very ruffled. What the hell did you say to him?
IRIS. I told you, just a few direct questions.
DAN. I guess that's what it takes. Did Scanlon call here to-
day? Reach said he talked to him last night.
IRIS. Yes, he called. He was ... reasonably supportive. He said
we should work the way we needed to.
DAN. Right up until he fires us. He didn't suggest how we
might keep Reach talking?
IRIS. That won't be a problem.
DAN. You're already banned. I could go any time.
IRIS. Reach'll get over this. He needs us.
DAN. He needs writers, not necessarily us. Scanlon can't do
anything if Reach won't talk to us — we'll have to be replaced.

IRIS. I just wanted the book to have some truth.

DAN. It's *got* the truth. It's fucking inundated with trut heard so much truth today I don't think I'll ever forgi myself. *(A beat.)* Tomorrow you need to go in there and apolo gize to Bill. That's if he'll even see you.

IRIS. I can't do that.

DAN. Then you'll wind up sitting here all day, writing down questions for me to go ask him. Is that what you want? *(A beat.)*

IRIS. What did Reach tell you, anyway?

DAN. What do you mean?

IRIS. What was the lower circle of hell?

DAN. Oh. It's on the tape. *(Lights shift to the interview room as she takes the briefcase and moves there.)*


## Scene 19

*Iris sits and turns on the tape. Reach is already sitting there.*


IRIS. Today I'd like to talk about your fourteenth, fifteenth and sixteenth victims. You killed them all the same night — is that right?

REACH. *(Sing-song.)* Say I'm sorry.

IRIS. In a period of about six hours. You drove all night that night?

REACH. Put on a lot of miles. Say I'm sorry.

IRIS. You know how I feel.

REACH. But you don't say it. Say it. *(A beat.)*

IRIS. I'm sorry.

REACH. Apology accepted.

IRIS. I'm sorry you don't want to talk about some very interesting material. Because God knows other people have, and will. Your point of view on this will never be heard.

REACH. That's right.

IRIS. Your fourteenth murder —

CH. Killing.

. Killing?

ACH. Murders have motives.

RIS. Took place early in the evening. You were on the road.

REACH. Stopped at a carnival. Saw a girl there —

IRIS. Diane McCusick.

REACH. I suppose. She was there with friends, but she'd lost track of 'em. Offered to walk around with her, look for 'em.

IRIS. She was twenty. College student? *(Reach stares at her.)*

REACH. We got out near the parking lot. I told her I had something that could alter her mood in my car, and ...

IRIS. How did you kill her?

REACH. Hit her, as soon as we were in the car.

IRIS. With what?

REACH. Hammer. Did them all with a hammer that night. It was an efficient evening.

IRIS. You didn't leave the bodies at Sugar Lake, even though it was close by. Why not?

REACH. It's kind of personal. Awhile before that, after I dumped the tenth one ... um, shit, um —

IRIS. Roberta Anson.

REACH. I realized I forgot something. A bracelet — ankle bracelet. I always took things like that, threw them somewhere else. Why make it easy? So one day I went back.

IRIS. In daylight?

REACH. It was raining. Figured it'd be safe. I got to the hill-side and looked down. She was lying there, but a lot further down. Animals had, you know, dragged her. I started down. It was slippery, and there was this smell. The rain kept it under control, but it was still ... I went down this slope —

IRIS. Past bodies?

REACH. Not there. Anyhow, I slipped. Slid all the way down, maybe thirty feet — covered in mud. Ended up right next to her body. Um, Roberta. And right there by my hand was her leg with the ankle bracelet. I tore it off and stood up, looked around — and all around me, everywhere, were these bodies. These parts of ... you know. And suddenly I saw this place for the first time. A place that I'd made. Sculpted. And I had this

urge. I didn't do it, but ... No. No, I did do it. I did dc
This would be good in a movie, too. I had this incredible urg
to howl. To just ... *(He trails off. We almost expect him to howl.)*
IRIS. You howled?
REACH. Yes. It was like a howl.
IRIS. Did you howl or didn't you? *(He stares at her.)*
REACH. I howled. *(A beat.)* I switched sites after that — got
worried about losing control. *(Iris takes the tape and briefcase and
moves into the motel. Lights shift with her.)*


## Scene 20

> *Dan sits looking out the motel window. Iris throws the brief-
> case on the bed. Afternoon.*

DAN. How was he?
IRIS. The usual unspeakable. We talked about Diane
McCusick, Beverly Flemming, Mary Lander.
DAN. Fourteen, fifteen, sixteen. Sounds like he accepted your
apology. *(She stares at him.)* Did he say anything about his mys-
tery victim?
IRIS. I really don't want to talk about it right now. *(Picking
up Dan's tape recorder.)* What did you do all day?
DAN. Oh — don't touch that. It's at a special place.
IRIS. Good. I'm dying to be at a special place. *(She turns it
on. He reaches for it.)*
DAN. No —
IRIS. *(Pulling it away.)* Share your day. *(On the tape we hear the
sound of vehicles roaring by on the Interstate.)* What is this?
DAN. Turn it off.
IRIS. *(Still listening to it.)* Did you record this?
DAN. It doesn't matter —
IRIS. What's it supposed to mean?
DAN. Nothing. I was bored.
IRIS. How much did you do?
DAN. Give it to me. *(He reaches for the tape, she avoids him, fast-*

*ards the tape.) Iris. (She turns it on again. Same sounds of ve-*
*les rushing along.)*

IRIS.   I don't believe this.

DAN.   There's nothing to believe —

IRIS.   *(Fast-forwarding again, turning it on to hear the same sounds.)*
Did you just go out by the highway and — ?

DAN.   *(Finally taking the tape recorder away.) It doesn't matter!!?
All right!? (He turns it off.)*

IRIS.   How long did you do this?

DAN.   Just today.

IRIS.   You spent a whole day on this?

DAN.   I wasted time. Yes, I wasted time. Take me out and
shoot me!

IRIS.   I only mean —

DAN.   *It is not easy to look out this window!* I have a right to
think about what I choose to think about! And I do not
choose to think about four million cubic yards of concrete
overpass. I do not choose to think about a shitpile of a house,
and most of all — most of all, Iris — I do not choose to think
about a fucking water heater!

IRIS.   Don't look at it, then! Don't look out this window, and
you won't see a — *(She stops short, looking out the window.)* It's
not there.

DAN.   Very good!

IRIS.   What did you do?

DAN.   I got rid of it.

IRIS.   How?

DAN.   I bought it. I went over there, said hi to Mrs. Pearson
— that's her name, by the way — and asked how much she
wanted for such an incomparable water heater. To which she
replied — and I could kiss her for this — "That piece of junk?
You can have it for the the price of hauling it away." Then I
used my investigative skills to find a junk-dealer in the phone
book, and lo and behold in twenty-three minutes he was there
with two fine, strapping assistants. And for less than the cost
of a day's parking in Manhattan, that water heater was in the
back of a truck, traveling deep into the dark folds of history.

IRIS.   You got rid of it.

DAN. *I got rid of it!* And then I missed it. And I spent all
sitting here trying not to feel more oppressed by its absen
than by its presence. And I started thinking about you, an
feeling regret — recalling that not really since the night you
did the travelogue have we — *(He stops himself.)* Which oddly
enough made me decide not to think about anything today,
so instead I taped some nearby authentic ambient sounds. And
I got carried away and ... spent all afternoon.
IRIS. Well. I'm glad you've had such a full, emotional day.
DAN. I'm being honest here.
IRIS. Fuck you.
DAN. Iris —
IRIS. I *liked* that water heater.
DAN. You were obsessed with it —
IRIS. *So what!?* At least I was obsessed with something harm-
less! Not like you, with all your lame notes about the highway
and coming to understand how a man can get sick enough to
kill nineteen perfect strangers —
DAN. Iris —
IRIS. *You sympathize with him!! It's in your notes!! (A beat.)* Is this
who I'm married to? Is this who I'm going to have a child
with?
DAN. *Maybe not! (A beat.)* This is getting to us. We wouldn't
be normal if this didn't get to us.
IRIS. We'll never be normal again. *(A beat.)* He's starting to
lie.
DAN. What?
IRIS. Reach. I caught him embellishing today. Making a de-
tail a little bit more terrible than it really was. I think he's
starting to figure something out.
DAN. What?
IRIS. That people want more. It makes him afraid.
DAN. Afraid?
IRIS. That he wasn't horrible enough.
DAN. I don't know what you're talking about.
IRIS. He's in prison. He reads the paper, sees movies-of-the-
week about men who kill thirty, forty — God knows how many
people. Who torture, mutilate with style. I think he's lying just

:ep up. *(A beat.)*

N. It doesn't matter.

JS. Doesn't matter?

JAN. It's his book. If he lies, and someday people uncover those lies, that's just another fact to know about him. Whatever comes out of his mouth, he's the primary source.

IRIS. And what are we? *(Lights fade to black.)*

## Scene 21

*Lights rise slowly on Iris and Reach, asleep on the bed. They're clothed, nuzzled together on top of the covers. They embrace and slowly kiss each other awake. The instant Iris realizes it's Reach, she jumps up.*

IRIS. *(Hesitating, staring at Reach.)* I wanted to prove ... I wanted to prove that I could listen to the worst crimes. That I could hear what killers did from the killers themselves. That I could face ... *(Moving away from Reach, looking out the window.)* That I could work with you, write the story without becoming.... *(A beat.)* I thought I could look at you for what you are: both a cause and a result, both human and ... something else. A final judgment, and a warning of something even more final. *(She looks at Reach.)* Part of me — as you were once, part of a woman — and part of nothing. That's all I wanted: to record each detail, one after another, no matter how ... foreign — without getting lost. And I could, once.

REACH. Before me.

IRIS. Before you. *(Lights fade to black.)*

# Scene 22

*Lights up to very bright on the interview room. Reach
across the table from both Iris and Dan. The tape is runnin.
Reach can't conceal a grin.*

IRIS. Jeannette Perry was ten.

REACH. That's right.

DAN. Wasn't that unusual for you?

REACH. Her age? Yeah.

IRIS. Where did you find her? *(Reach laughs.)*

DAN. Bill, what's wrong?

REACH. What do you mean?

DAN. Why are you laughing?

REACH. Feels strange having you both here. Don't get me
wrong, you look cute. But why the switch? Safety in numbers?

IRIS. Bill, where did you find Jeannette Perry?

REACH. At her school. There was a convenience store about
a block away. Kids went back and forth.

DAN. She was alone?

REACH. Yeah.

DAN. And you —

REACH. Grabbed her.

IRIS. Didn't she yell?

REACH. Sure. Couple kids heard, but they were pretty far off.
Everyone else was in the store. I pulled her around the cor-
ner, threw her in my car, drove off. The way I went, no one
could see the car. You guys look exactly like a couple I knew
in high school.

IRIS. Grabbing her like that seems reckless.

REACH. I broke every rule in the book. Should've been
caught. That couple — what the hell were they voted? Most
likely to have a baby or something, I can't remember. *(Iris looks
at Dan, who hurries to the next question.)*

DAN. Why a little girl?

REACH. What? Oh — I couldn't go any longer.

DAN. You mean the compulsion — ?

47

That's right.
.o, anybody — any woman, girl — ?
. Hey, what are you going to call it?
. Bill —
5. Call what?
AN. We're not here to talk about —
REACH. You guys'll make great parents.
IRIS. *(To Dan.)* You told him?
DAN. It slipped out one day. I'm sorry.
IRIS. It slipped out?
REACH. I hope it's a girl. Women like girls.
IRIS. Shut up.
DAN. Iris — !
IRIS. How could you — ?!
DAN. I said I'm sorry!
IRIS. That's not good enough!
REACH. It's just a baby —
IRIS. *Why did you kill a ten-year-old!?*
REACH. *I felt like it! (Sharp rapping at the door. All three wave it away simultaneously.)* I didn't like killing her that way. Don't like being that out of control. It's nothing I'm proud of.
IRIS. It's nothing you're proud of? *(A beat.)* So, you weren't functioning as a human being then, right?
REACH. What?
IRIS. I mean, there wouldn't've been any higher brain function connected with this sort of activity, would there?
DAN. Iris —
IRIS. Any animal, any species that preys on the untended young of its own kind would be capable of doing what you did. *(Reach suddenly turns off the tape.)*
REACH. What kind of comment is that?
DAN. She doesn't mean it.
REACH. Are you calling me subhuman? Is that how you're going to explain things? That I'm subhuman?
DAN. We're not going to explain things at all. That's not our job.
REACH. Damn right it's not. *(To Iris.)* Right? *(A beat. Dan turns on the tape.)*

48

IRIS. Why are you subhuman?

REACH. *GODDAMMIT — !!* (*Reach rises threateningly rapping at the door. Reach shouts furiously.*) *EVERYTHING'S _ING GREAT!!* (*The rapping suddenly stops. Reach speaks in a mal tone.*) It's because it's a kid, isn't it? Take six or seven ye off a victim and you can't hear about it. I'll tell you somethin. — it's the same life. Ten, twenty, boy, girl — same life. We've all got one, and right now people want to hear about mine. Jeannette Perry's part of my life. It didn't have to be her, but it had to be someone. Finally, there had to be a girl. And I had to kill her.

IRIS. So you could tell your story?

REACH. You know how many kids are born in this country every minute? Let's say one was born right ... (*Pointing at Dan's watch.*) ... now — ok? Then the next one would be born right about — (*Pointing at the watch each time he says "now."*) ... now. And the next one — would come along right ... now. And it goes on like this — here comes the next one right ...

DAN. Jeannette Perry.

REACH. ... Now — twenty-four hours a day, seven days a week, twelve months a year —

DAN. You killed her.

REACH. Now.

DAN. Right away?

REACH. No.

DAN. No? But the court record said —

REACH. I lied. Made the case simpler. Easier on everybody. (*Reach moves into the motel. Lights are up on both rooms.*)

DAN. You buried Jeannette's body and covered it with quick-lime. It was quite ... decomposed when it was found. Are you saying that you — ?

REACH. I put a loop around her neck.

DAN. To choke her?

REACH. Her breath was coming real fast. I didn't look at her face. Just listened to her breath. It was like the air was forcing itself into her, whether she wanted it to or not.

IRIS. (*Quietly.*) He's lying.

DAN. Then what did you do?

I confessed. I told her what I'd done. Victim by vic-

How many were there?

. He's *lying*.

ACH. I was looking past her, out the car window. There
as a little brown bird sitting real close, on a stump. The kind
of bird you'd never notice in a whole lifetime. And I held on
to that loop, and told my story, and the air was roaring in and
out of her by now, so loud that.... And then it touched me.
On my neck — I felt her breath, it.... And I looked up, and
I pulled on the loop hard — like I was trying to pull someone up over a cliff, and ... her eyes were all I could see. They
looked grateful. They got bluer and bluer, until finally they
went the deep blue the sky turns just before it's night. *(Iris
takes a small piece of paper from the briefcase and puts it in her
pocket. She moves into the motel room.)*
IRIS. Eventually you gave yourself up. You walked into a
county sheriff's office and confessed. Why?
REACH. It was time.
IRIS. Time to quit? Or announce what you'd done?
REACH. Both. *(Iris pulls the piece of paper from her pocket.)*
IRIS. This is a picture of Jeannette Perry. Her fifth-grade
school photo. Scanlon wants to use it in the book. Any prob-
lems with it?
REACH. *(Looking at it.)* No.
IRIS. Her eyes are brown. *(She tears the picture in two, throws
the pieces at Reach. Dan rushes into the motel room.)*
DAN. *Iris* — !
REACH. So I forgot. It doesn't prove anything. *(Smiling, Reach
moves away from them.)*
DAN. We agreed. We agreed to try this.
IRIS. Why? To give him a voice? *Him?*
DAN. He has a right to tell his story.
IRIS. The right to tell any story — that's what we're giving
him. You know what else we're giving him? The right to cover-
art. On a million paperbacks, all over the country. It'll be just
his eyes — staring out from over the title: *Blood Sport* or *Blood
For Me*, or —

REACH. *Blood Hunger.* I've decided. *(Reach is by now*
*his back on the bed. He has removed his handcuffs — simp*
*them off — and idly plays with them as Dan and Iris argue.*
IRIS. Staring out from the shelves of every drugstore
supermarket. Saying, "Look at me — Bill Reach. I'm m
important than you."
DAN. He is. What he did is. It's more socially significant —
it deserves to be studied.
IRIS. It isn't studied, it's consumed.
DAN. So what?! That's how we do it here. He kills people —
we put him on the news. He's fascinating — we write about
him.
REACH. That's true.
DAN. When someone like him is discovered —
IRIS. *Chooses* to be discovered.
DAN. We discuss him in as broad a forum as possible. Lear-
nedly, scientifically, foolishly, crassly, pervertedly — every way.
Every way. That's what this culture does.
IRIS. Nineteen slaughtered girls: that's what this culture does.
And it does one more thing. It charges admission.
DAN. Iris —
IRIS. We promote it! We do. We make it more likely — not
less — that this'll happen to someone else's daughter. To *our*
daughter —
DAN. For Christ's sake, you're not even discussing this any-
more.
IRIS. What are you doing? Apologizing for — apologizing *to*
— Bill Reach, trying to understand Bill Reach, for all I know
trying to become Bill Reach —
REACH. There's only one Bill Reach.
DAN. I'm *trying* to finish what I start. I'm trying not to walk
away from the book of my career. *Our* career. I'm trying to
stay with this long enough to find out who Reach's other vic-
tim is!
IRIS. I know who it is.
DAN. You do?! Who?
IRIS. It's you. *(A beat.)*
DAN. There's a dead woman out there. Somewhere. Only he

...er parents, whoever they are, don't know what hap-
...They'll never know unless someone talks to Bill Reach
...ess someone gives him a reason to talk. He may tell lies
...t her. He may feed our nightmares. He may like it. But
...y he can walk out into a field — *somewhere* — and give us
...ck what's left of her.

IRIS. *(A beat.)* I'm going. *(She moves to leave.)*

DAN. Iris, don't.

IRIS. Come with me.

DAN. I can't do that.

IRIS. I can't stay. *(She starts out again.)*

DAN. Iris — !

REACH. She'll stay. All I've got to say is Renee Michaels.
*(Reach locks the handcuffs back onto his wrists and sits up on the
edge of the bed. Iris stops. They stare at Reach.)*

DAN. Who's that?

REACH. Someone I killed.

DAN. She's not one of the nineteen.

REACH. She's from before. She's extra. *(Dan hesitates, then
moves to set up a tape recorder on the bed.)* You didn't think I'd
leave you high and dry? I'll add a new killing. Got to sell this
thing. There's plenty of competition out there.

DAN. Iris?

REACH. It's an exclusive.

DAN. *(Turning on the tape.)* This person's name was Renee
Michaels?

REACH. Yes. No one's found her yet. I buried her.

DAN. Do you remember where?

REACH. Absolutely.

DAN. Iris? Iris? *(To Reach.)* So her family, for example, still
doesn't know — for sure — even that she's dead?

REACH. Not until right now.

DAN. Iris? *(Slowly Iris moves to the interview room and sits. She
stares at them in the motel room.)* How old was Renee Michaels?

REACH. Eighteen.

DAN. Where did you meet her?

REACH. In a bar.

DAN. Near your home? *(Lights on the motel room begin a slow*

.52

*fade.)*
REACH. Yeah, pretty close.
DAN. Was she someone you knew?
REACH. I'd never seen her before in my life. *(Lights fade on Dan and Reach in the motel, but stay up on Iris. Her sta hasn't changed. After a moment a rapping is heard — steady, no sharp. She doesn't move. The rapping comes again. She doesn't move. Lights fade to black.)*

**THE END**

# PROPERTY LIST

etter to fan (Reach)
Letter to Reach from fan (Reach)
Snapshot of Reach's fan (Reach)
Black briefcase (Dan)
   inside:  notepad
           few pens
           papers in folder
Notepad (Dan)
Maroon briefcase (Iris)
   inside:  notepad
           few pens
           photograph of victim
2 pens (Dan)
Handcuffs (Reach)
2 tape recorders (Dan, Iris)
   cassettes for recorders (Dan, Iris)
   batteries for recorders (Dan, Iris)
Snapshot of Reach in college
4 notepads
3 pens

# COSTUME PLOT

**Dan Henniman**
White cotton singlet undershirt
Khaki pants
3 cotton pullover shirts
Green and black houndstooth jacket
Brown cotton socks
Brown loafers
Olive canvas belt
Watch
Wedding band
White cotton handkerchief

**Iris Henniman**
Bra
Panties
Black wool pants
Turquoise blouse
Taupe jacket
Black knee-hi's
Brown leather shoes
Black leather belt
Gold earrings
Wrist watch
Wedding band

**William Reach**
White cotton crew neck t-shirt
Blue chambray work shirt
Washed jeans
White tube socks
Brown boots

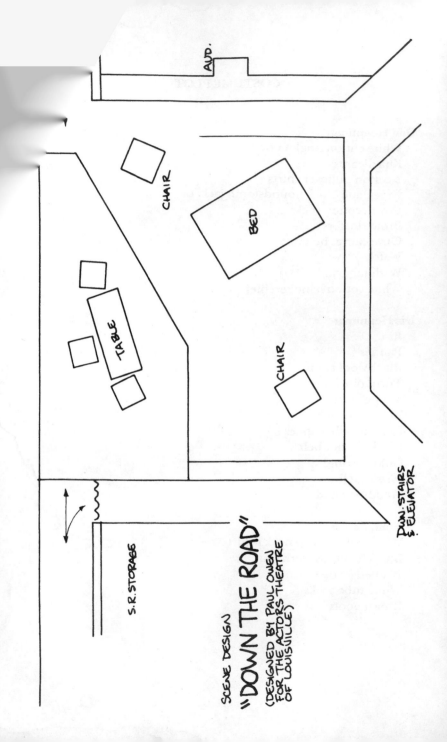

SCENE DESIGN
"DOWN THE ROAD"

(DESIGNED BY PAUL OWEN
FOR THE ACTORS THEATRE
OF LOUISVILLE)

S.R. STORAGE

TABLE

CHAIR

CHAIR

BED

AUD.

DWN. STAIRS
& ELEVATOR

# NEW PLAYS

★ **YELLOW FACE by David Henry Hwang.** Asian-American playw
DHH leads a protest against the casting of Jonathan Pryce as the Eurasian pr.
in the original Broadway production of *Miss Saigon*, condemning the practice
"yellowface." The lines between truth and fiction blur with hilarious and moving results in this unreliable memoir. "A pungent play of ideas with a big heart."
–*Variety*. "Fabulously inventive." –*The New Yorker*. [5M, 2W] ISBN: 978-0-
8222-2301-6

★ **33 VARIATIONS by Moisés Kaufmann.** A mother coming to terms with
her daughter. A composer coming to terms with his genius. And, even though
they're separated by 200 years, these two people share an obsession that might,
even just for a moment, make time stand still. "A compellingly original and
thoroughly watchable play for today." –*Talkin' Broadway*. [4M, 4W] ISBN:
978-0-8222-2392-4

★ **BOOM by Peter Sinn Nachtrieb.** A grad student's online personal ad lures
a mysterious journalism student to his subterranean research lab. But when a
major catastrophic event strikes the planet, their date takes on evolutionary sig-
nificance and the fate of humanity hangs in the balance. "Darkly funny dialogue." –*NY Times*. "Literate, coarse, thoughtful, sweet, scabrously inappropri-
ate." –*Washington City Paper*. [1M, 2W] ISBN: 978-0-8222-2370-2

★ **LOVE, LOSS AND WHAT I WORE by Nora Ephron and Delia Ephron,
based on the book by Ilene Beckerman.** A play of monologues and ensem-
ble pieces about women, clothes and memory covering all the important subjects—mothers, prom dresses, mothers, buying bras, mothers, hating purses
and why we only wear black. "Funny, compelling." –*NY Times*. "So funny and
so powerful." –*WowOwow.com*. [5W] ISBN: 978-0-8222-2355-9

★ **CIRCLE MIRROR TRANSFORMATION by Annie Baker.** When four
lost New Englanders enrolled in Marty's community center drama class exper-
iment with harmless games, hearts are quietly torn apart, and tiny wars of epic
proportions are waged and won. "Absorbing, unblinking and sharply funny."
–*NY Times*. [2M, 3W] ISBN: 978-0-8222-2445-7

★ **BROKE-OLOGY by Nathan Louis Jackson.** The King family has weath-
ered the hardships of life and survived with their love for each other intact. But
when two brothers are called home to take care of their father, they find themselves strangely at odds. "Engaging dialogue." –*TheaterMania.com*. "Assured,
bighearted." –*Time Out*. [3M, 1W] ISBN: 978-0-8222-2428-0

**DRAMATISTS PLAY SERVICE, INC.**
**440 Park Avenue South, New York, NY 10016  212-683-8960  Fax 212-213-1539**
postmaster@dramatists.com  www.dramatists.com

# NEW PLAYS

CIVIL WAR CHRISTMAS: AN AMERICAN MUSICAL CELEBRA-
TION by Paula Vogel, music by Daryl Waters. It's 1864, and Washington,
D.C. is settling down to the coldest Christmas Eve in years. Intertwining many
lives, this musical shows us that the gladness of one's heart is the best gift of all.
"Boldly inventive theater, warm and affecting." –*Talkin' Broadway.* "Crisp strokes
of dialogue." –*NY Times.* [12M, 5W] ISBN: 978-0-8222-2361-0

★ SPEECH & DEBATE by Stephen Karam. Three teenage misfits in Salem,
Oregon discover they are linked by a sex scandal that's rocked their town. "Savvy
comedy." –*Variety.* "Hilarious, cliché-free, and immensely entertaining." –*NY
Times.* "A strong, rangy play." –*NY Newsday.* [2M, 2W] ISBN: 978-0-8222-
2286-6

★ DIVIDING THE ESTATE by Horton Foote. Matriarch Stella Gordon is
determined not to divide her 100-year-old Texas estate, despite her family's
declining wealth and the looming financial crisis. But her three children have
another plan. "Goes for laughs and succeeds." –*NY Daily News.* "The theatrical
equivalent of a page-turner." –*Bloomberg.com.* [4M, 9W] ISBN: 978-0-8222-
2398-6

★ WHY TORTURE IS WRONG, AND THE PEOPLE WHO LOVE
THEM by Christopher Durang. Christopher Durang turns political humor
upside down with this raucous and provocative satire about America's growing
homeland "insecurity." "A smashing new play." –*NY Observer.* "You may laugh
yourself silly." –*Bloomberg News.* [4M, 3W] ISBN: 978-0-8222-2401-3

★ FIFTY WORDS by Michael Weller. While their nine-year-old son is away
for the night on his first sleepover, Adam and Jan have an evening alone together,
beginning a suspenseful nightlong roller-coaster ride of revelation, rancor, passion and humor. "Mr. Weller is a bold and productive dramatist." –*NY Times.*
[1M, 1W] ISBN: 978-0-8222-2348-1

★ BECKY'S NEW CAR by Steven Dietz. Becky Foster is caught in middle age,
middle management and in a middling marriage—with no prospects for change
on the horizon. Then one night a socially inept and grief-struck millionaire stum-
bles into the car dealership where Becky works. "Gently and consistently funny."
–*Variety.* "Perfect blend of hilarious comedy and substantial weight." –*Broadway
Hour.* [4M, 3W] ISBN: 978-0-8222-2393-1

**DRAMATISTS PLAY SERVICE, INC.**
440 Park Avenue South, New York, NY 10016 212-683-8960 Fax 212-213-1539
postmaster@dramatists.com www.dramatists.com

# NEW PLAYS

★ **AT HOME AT THE ZOO by Edward Albee.** Edward Albee delves deeper into his play THE ZOO STORY by adding a first act, HOMELIFE, which precedes Peter's fateful meeting with Jerry on a park bench in Central Park. "An essential and heartening experience." –*NY Times.* "Darkly comic and thrilling." –*Time Out.* "Genuinely fascinating." –*Journal News.* [2M, 1W] ISBN: 978-0-8222-2317-7

★ **PASSING STRANGE book and lyrics by Stew, music by Stew and Heidi Rodewald, created in collaboration with Annie Dorsen.** A daring musical about a young bohemian that takes you from black middle-class America to Amsterdam, Berlin and beyond on a journey towards personal and artistic authenticity. "Fresh, exuberant, bracingly inventive, bitingly funny, and full of heart." –*NY Times.* "The freshest musical in town!" –*Wall Street Journal.* "Excellent songs and a vulnerable heart." –*Variety.* [4M, 3W] ISBN: 978-0-8222-2400-6

★ **REASONS TO BE PRETTY by Neil LaBute.** Greg really, truly adores his girlfriend, Steph. Unfortunately, he also thinks she has a few physical imperfections, and when he mentions them, all hell breaks loose. "Tight, tense and emotionally true." –*Time Magazine.* "Lively and compulsively watchable." –*The Record.* [2M, 2W] ISBN: 978-0-8222-2394-8

★ **OPUS by Michael Hollinger.** With only a few days to rehearse a grueling Beethoven masterpiece, a world-class string quartet struggles to prepare their highest-profile performance ever—a televised ceremony at the White House. "Intimate, intense and profoundly moving." –*Time Out.* "Worthy of scores of bravissimos." –*BroadwayWorld.com.* [4M, 1W] ISBN: 978-0-8222-2363-4

★ **BECKY SHAW by Gina Gionfriddo.** When an evening calculated to bring happiness takes a dark turn, crisis and comedy ensue in this wickedly funny play that asks what we owe the people we love and the strangers who land on our doorstep. "As engrossing as it is ferociously funny." –*NY Times.* "Gionfriddo is some kind of genius." –*Variety.* [2M, 3W] ISBN: 978-0-8222-2402-0

★ **KICKING A DEAD HORSE by Sam Shepard.** Hobart Struther's horse has just dropped dead. In an eighty-minute monologue, he discusses what path brought him here in the first place, the fate of his marriage, his career, politics and eventually the nature of the universe. "Deeply instinctual and intuitive." –*NY Times.* "The brilliance is in the infinite reverberations Shepard extracts from his simple metaphor." –*TheaterMania.* [1M, 1W] ISBN: 978-0-8222-2336-8

**DRAMATISTS PLAY SERVICE, INC.**
440 Park Avenue South, New York, NY 10016  212-683-8960  Fax 212-213-1539
postmaster@dramatists.com   www.dramatists.com

# NEW PLAYS

**AUGUST: OSAGE COUNTY by Tracy Letts.** WINNER OF THE 2008 ULITZER PRIZE AND TONY AWARD. When the large Weston family reunites after Dad disappears, their Oklahoma homestead explodes in a maelstrom of repressed truths and unsettling secrets. "Fiercely funny and bitingly sad." *–NY Times.* "Ferociously entertaining." *–Variety.* "A hugely ambitious, highly combustible saga." *–NY Daily News.* [6M, 7W] ISBN: 978-0-8222-2300-9

★ **RUINED by Lynn Nottage.** WINNER OF THE 2009 PULITZER PRIZE. Set in a small mining town in Democratic Republic of Congo, RUINED is a haunting, probing work about the resilience of the human spirit during times of war. "A full-immersion drama of shocking complexity and moral ambiguity." *–Variety.* "Sincere, passionate, courageous." *–Chicago Tribune.* [8M, 4W] ISBN: 978-0-8222-2390-0

★ **GOD OF CARNAGE by Yasmina Reza, translated by Christopher Hampton.** WINNER OF THE 2009 TONY AWARD. A playground altercation between boys brings together their Brooklyn parents, leaving the couples in tatters as the rum flows and tensions explode. "Satisfyingly primitive entertainment." *–NY Times.* "Elegant, acerbic, entertainingly fueled on pure bile." *–Variety.* [2M, 2W] ISBN: 978-0-8222-2399-3

★ **THE SEAFARER by Conor McPherson.** Sharky has returned to Dublin to look after his irascible, aging brother. Old drinking buddies Ivan and Nicky are holed up at the house too, hoping to play some cards. But with the arrival of a stranger from the distant past, the stakes are raised ever higher. "Dark and enthralling Christmas fable." *–NY Times.* "A timeless classic." *–Hollywood Reporter.* [5M] ISBN: 978-0-8222-2284-2

★ **THE NEW CENTURY by Paul Rudnick.** When the playwright is Paul Rudnick, expectations are geared for a play both hilarious and smart, and this provocative and outrageous comedy is no exception. "The one-liners fly like rockets." *–NY Times.* "The funniest playwright around." *–Journal News.* [2M, 3W] ISBN: 978-0-8222-2315-3

★ **SHIPWRECKED! AN ENTERTAINMENT—THE AMAZING ADVENTURES OF LOUIS DE ROUGEMONT (AS TOLD BY HIMSELF) by Donald Margulies.** The amazing story of bravery, survival and celebrity that left nineteenth-century England spellbound. Dare to be whisked away. "A deft, literate narrative." *–LA Times.* "Springs to life like a theatrical pop-up book." *–NY Times.* [2M, 1W] ISBN: 978-0-8222-2341-2

**DRAMATISTS PLAY SERVICE, INC.**
440 Park Avenue South, New York, NY 10016  212-683-8960  Fax 212-213-1539
postmaster@dramatists.com  www.dramatists.com